One day you finally knew
what you had to do, and began...
and there was a new voice
which you slowly
recognized as your own,
that kept you company
as you strode deeper and deeper
into the world,
determined to do
the only thing you could do —
determined to save
the only life you could save.

Mary Oliver

Also by Brian Browne Walker

I Ching

Tao Te Ching

Hua–Hu Ching: The Unknown Teachings of Lao Tzu

The Crazy Dog Guide to Lifetime Happiness

The Crazy Dog Guide to Happier Work

Be Happy Now

BRIAN BROWNE WALKER

BeHappyBooks.com

behappybooks.com
Post Office Box 422
Boulder, Colorado 80306

ISBN #0-9749422-0-0
First Edition

this book is livicated to happiness,
to those who are participating in it,
and to those who wish to join us —
come on in, the water is great.

Table of Contents

A note about the use of the word "God".

You will see the word "God" from time to time in this book. I use it because it works for me in capturing the essence of a very high ideal, but I encourage you to freely substitute any word or phrase that works better for you — "my higher self", "the greatest good", love", "the great and powerful Oz" — whatever you like.

They're all good.

We'll find out down the road what the true name and nature of our Creator is. In the meantime, please feel free to use the one that suits you best.

This is the simplest book in the world
about how to use
the most powerful tools in the world
to create the rarest thing in the world:

genuine,
lasting happiness
and success.

If you use what I'm teaching in this book,
I guarantee that you will achieve it.

And if you don't use what's taught here — whether
you learn it from me, or from someone else —
I can pretty much guarantee that you won't.

So before you go on, ask yourself this question:

"Do I absolutely, positively want to become
a truly, deeply, authentically, permanently
happy and successful person?

If the answer is emphatically "Yes!", then read on.

If it isn't, you'd better stop now

Because what's in this book is contagious.

Life is wonderful.
Why are so many folks so unhappy?

The ease and gentility of modern Western life would astound our ancestors. Ours is not a perfect world, but just in the last hundred years, we have nearly doubled the average lifespan, eradicated most of the plagues that haunted us, drastically reduced our vulnerability to infectious diseases, and learned to work half as much time as our great-grandparents used to, at significantly gentler labors, for vastly greater rewards. We communicate around the globe in milliseconds and travel to any spot on it in less than a day from the comfortable, well-lit homes that we own. Access to education and culture in myriad forms is widespread and largely affordable, and our level of political, religious, sexual, and every other kind of freedom is absolutely unprecedented. Telemarketers and pop-up ads aside, we live in Paradise.

But do we feel good about the era in which we live or hold the view that life is getting better? That's not what we tell the people who poll us. We tell them that things are getting worse, that our ancestors had it better than we do, that we're stressed out, and that our children are in for a hard time.

Here is a sad but fascinating fact: The percentage of people in the Western world — America, western Europe, and Japan — who describe themselves as "happy" is exactly the same as it was over fifty years ago, in spite of the fact that life in all of those places has grown better in all the ways described above. Not only that, but the incidence of depression has risen by a factor of ten in the same period of time.

What does this tell us? It tells us that people in general either have an inclination toward happiness, or away from it, and what's going on in the world around them doesn't really affect them all that much.

Yea, verily, not even the rich are happy. Numerous social scientists have studied the relationship between money and happiness carefully, and this is what they've concluded: there isn't one. In spite of our culture's obsession with wealth and all its trappings, the fact is that once a person has a minimal "safety net" level of income — something to eat and wear, and a roof of some sort overhead — the amount of money he or she possesses beyond that has *absolutely no bearing* on his or her level of personal happiness. None. Believe it or not, it's a scientifically researched and documented fact that millionaires and lottery winners are no happier than the rest of us.

Again, what does all this tell us? *It tells us that people in general either have an inclination toward happiness, or away from it, and what's going on in the world around them doesn't really affect them all that much. Remember this!*

Happiness doesn't come from the outside.

This book is about where happiness does come from, and how you can get it and keep it by applying seven simple principles in your daily living that are *absolutely proven to work*.

If you are anything like me, you're now wondering, Who is this guy? Where did these principles come from? Is this a religion? And what's it gonna cost me?"

The answers are: I'll tell you who I am as we go; I got these principles partly from the school of hard knocks, and partly from some people who are or were highly adept at the art of living; no, not a religion, unless it's a religion of kindness; and your total cost is the price of this book. And if you buy the book and apply the principles, and it doesn't work for you, I'll give you your money back.

I wrote this book because I used to be miserable.

Despite being born free, white, male, middle class, reasonably good looking, athletic, healthy, and intelligent — all supposed advantages in this world — and then given a decent education and some love and some opportunities in life, I nonetheless passed the better part of four decades on this gorgeous garden planet in a state of fairly regular, and sometimes quite advanced, unhappiness. I banked money, climbed mountains, made love with beautiful and extraordinary women, published books and wrote screenplays — and suffered.

And I finally got tired of suffering, and turned all my attention on it, and fixed it. Now I'm happy. And if *you* are miserable now, or just habitually less than happy, I want to offer some help. I'm going to show you in no uncertain terms how you can be happy, too, and I *absolutely guarantee* that it will work for you, now and forevermore — whatever the conditions of your life are at this moment — if you'll apply yourself.

the best way to make your dreams come true is to wake up.

Paul Valery

Let's begin.

Chapter One

Valence is everything. Be positive.

Those five words up there? That's the master principle — heck, that's really the whole book. And you paid all that money for it! How do you feel about that?

It's not a frivolous question; I really mean it: Are you satisfied if the only thing you get out of this book is a strong black and white reminder to establish and maintain a positive outlook and attitude for the rest of your life? Are you thinking, "I've been fleeced!", or are you thinking, "Thank God you reminded me!" Your answer will tell you something about your valence. (By the way, there's a lot more in the book, if it's any consolation).

What is "valence", anyway? Webster's says that it's pronounced "VAY-lentz", it has its roots in a Latin word having to do with power, capacity, and strength (remember that!), and defines it this way:

> 1: the degree of combining power of an element...
> 2 a: relative capacity to unite, react, or interact...
> 2 b: the degree of attractiveness an individual, activity, or object possesses...

It's usually used as a scientific term, then, referring to the capacity of an element to combine and create strong interactions with other molecules. What *we* mean by it here is this: Are you attracted, drawn, and driven to unite with positive thoughts, feelings, people, and experiences, or negative ones? Are you a positive person, or a negative one? Are you negatively valent, or positively valent?

Stop.

Take a careful, quiet look
inside, and answer
the question:
are you
positive?

I made my own discovery about valence after a long dark period in my adult life, a period in which I gradually became completely and relentlessly negative about almost everything. I had good reasons, if you believe that there can be good reasons for taking such a self-destructive attitude: I was poor, divorced, depressed, entering middle age, raising my daughter alone with no help and lots of harm from her mother. I drove a twenty year old car. I had a big shot agent and wrote a bunch of screenplays that everyone in Hollywood loved but wouldn't make. I did a long interview on NPR about a new book I'd written, and people were lining up to buy it, but unbeknownst to me, the publisher was going bankrupt and hadn't reordered further printings. By the time that got sorted out, nobody knew who I was or wanted to buy my book anymore.

I had a knee that had been operated on three times, a bum shoulder, graying hair, no sweetheart, and all too often, a beer in one hand and a cigarette in the other. Oh, I still worked out every day, kept my house clean, made my daughter laugh, hugged my dog, worked on writing projects. But in my mind and heart, it was *all* beer and cigarettes. I was sad about everything, pissed off at everyone, mean, frowning, and frumpy.

And then one day — after, oh, nearly a decade like that — it dawned on me. I realized — subtly, quietly, in the privacy of my own mind and heart — that I had become a deeply, habitually, *religiously* negative person. (If you're thinking,

"*That* took a decade?", well, fair enough. But some folks *never* get it, so I actually feel fortunate.) In that moment, also quietly but with great clarity, I also saw where that negativity was going to take my life: into more of the same, and worse, and absolutely nowhere else. I saw clearly:

Nothing I want can come from this.

Nothing good could get in. Nobody good would *want* in. If hell is pain and unhappiness without chance of release, I had ridden negativity into hell. I understood that I had a serious valence problem, and I resolved then and there to change mine from negative to positive.

You carry heaven and
hell with you.
Ramana Maharshi

I want to emphasize to you that I'm talking about something subtle, something that, for me, happened in stillness. I did not get "saved" in a church ceremony. I didn't get in a car accident, die, walk toward the light, and get escorted back, healed, by angels. I didn't attend a personal growth seminar and publicly shout a pledge that "Every day, in every way, I'm getting better and better!" Not that there's a thing in the world wrong with any of those — they just didn't happen to me. I simply saw myself as I was, truly kenned the problem, and very quietly determined that I would not carry my negativity another step into the rest of my life or the lives of those close to me. I promised myself, in that moment, that I was going to do everything I could to make my valence positive: to make my every thought, action, and attitude positive from that day forward into forever. I want to stress to you that *I did not know what would happen as a result* — I was just determined to find out.

I must tell you also that outwardly, for some time afterward, nothing particularly spectacular happened. I was pretty much as I'd been before — broke, beat up, and alone. But inwardly, in that very moment, I actually felt my life begin to change.

What I felt was subtle but sure. I *knew* in my heart that I had a new life. I didn't have any more inkling than I'd had the day before about where my life would lead — didn't know if I'd ever feel good in my busted old athlete's body again, be married to someone I loved and admired and who loved and admired me, any of the things I so deeply desired — but I knew that it was going to be good *because I was determined to make it good*. And I have. And it is. And that doesn't mean that I'm now Rich Smart Pretty Most Popular Boy, with the body of Batman, and sleeping next to Catwoman, because I'm not. My life doesn't look entirely different — unless you're looking out of my eyes, thinking my thoughts, and feeling my feelings. In that regard, I'm Albert Einstein Pitt-Gates in a cape.

The greatest treasure next to God
is a good will in this world:
Even if all has been lost,
by it all can be regained.
Angelus Silesius

I'm going to shut up about myself now and take you into the world of science for a moment, into a new school of thought known as Positive Psychology. Positive Psychology concerns itself with how people can and do increase their well-being through the establishment and exercise of strengths and virtues. In the old days, I'd never heard of it, which shouldn't surprise anyone — it couldn't get in! But not long after I changed my valence, I came across the work of Dr. Martin Seligman.

Dr. Seligman is a professor of psychology at the University of Pennsylvania, a past president of the 160,000 member American Psychological Association, and the author of twenty books. Well along into an accomplished career in the field of psychology, Dr. Seligman began to focus his attention on the fact that psychology has always, and virtually exclusively, concerned itself with illness, and not with wellness — "just how to go from minus five to minus three and feel a little less miserable day by day", as he puts it, rather than "how to go from plus two to plus seven in your life." (Psychologists and psychiatrists have a giant reference manual, the DSM, to describe the many and various negative states of the psyche — mental illnesses, in other words — and none to describe the positive!)

So Seligman redirected his labors into the field now known as Positive Psychology, where he learned what you're about to learn:

> It is in the *self-interest* of human beings to cultivate a positive, optimistic, grateful, and forgiving attitude. It is good for *you* — never mind the effect on others — to have a positive valence!

The scientific studies of others in the field, like Barbara Frederickson, a professor at the University of Michigan, and Lisa Aspinwall, a professor at the University of Utah, show convincingly that

positive emotions have
a hugely important
purpose in
evolution

They strengthen us in every way, making us more intellectually flexible and adept, better decision-makers, physically stronger, and better connected socially — all resources that we use and need in a time of trial or opportunity. In other

ur valence is positive today, you'll be more
ıorrow when the going gets tough, or gets good.
Seligman explains in his book Authentic
ositive feelings function as a set of neon indica-
, "Growth found here!" When our minds are
open, tolerant, and benevolent, we become mentally creative and physically and emotionally well. Positive people are not only measurably healthier and happier than others, but much better problem solvers as well. Dwelling in positive emotion simply improves every aspect of our social, intellectual, and physical lives. It's a scientific fact:

The evidence from dozens of rigorous studies conducted by psychologists and other social scientists is clear and consistent: positive thought, action, and orientation pay enormous dividends to those who habitually cultivate them.

And if you'd like a bit of evidence from the other side of the coin, consider the phenomenon of Moebius syndrome. Moebius syndrome is a form of facial paralysis that leaves its victims physically unable to smile or otherwise show positive emotion. Whatever their internal feelings are, Moebius sufferers react to even the happiest and friendliest conversations with a disconcerting deadpan. As a result they have tremendous difficulty making and keeping even casual friendships and romantic relationships.

You can't make friend with frowns.

For anyone who remains unconvinced, I highly recommend a full reading of *Authentic Happiness*. But do you really have to look to science books? I suggest that you look instead to your own life. You know this: When your valence is negative, the world is a nightmare — nothing good can get in, nobody loves you, and if someone gave you a Ferrari, you'd immediately find a flawed seam in the upholstery and be mad about it. When your valence is positive, on the other hand, the world is your oyster. You smile, make friends, and love everything — a bit of sunshine or a laugh with your kid is glorious indeed, and everything beyond just drawing breath is gravy.

When you smile, the world smiles with you.

The most powerful thing you can ever do in this life for yourself, your loved ones, and the world around you is establish, cultivate, and permanently maintain a positive valence. You'll be challenged, sure — the world is full of encouragements for you to feel wronged and aggrieved, get angry and vengeful, file lawsuits, throw punches, and spew venom. And, indeed, every *great* once in a while, you'll encounter someone or something that's so abjectly negative that all you can do is neutralize the situation by banishing him, her, or it from your life. But that's rare, and the truth is that once you have determined that you are going to live a positive life, nothing can stop you. Things will slow you down, sure — challenges from your friends and family, assaults on your valence from the outside world, snipers from your own long established negative thoughts, habits, and patterns.

Maintain your positive valence,
and every negative influence
in the world
will wither,
recede,
and drop away.

What follows this and each of the other chapters in this book is a garden of quotes on the subject at hand. These are things that others have said, in this case about the power of the positive, that you can use. Keep this book open to a quote you like, and keep it in front of you as you go through your day, and it will help you to be positive, happy, healthy, and strong. And remember that definition from Webster's. Positive valence is power, capacity to unite and interact, and attractiveness. Go get it.

great is the **human** who has not lost his **childlike heart.**

Mencius

life can only be understood backwards, but it must be lived forwards.

Soren Kierkegaard

we can easily **forgive** a **child** who is afraid of the **dark**; the **real** tragedy of **life** is when **adults** are **afraid** of the light.

Plato

hope begins in the dark, the stubborn hope that if you just show up and try to do the right thing, the dawn will come. you wait and watch and work: you don't give up.

Anne Lamott

say yes when nobody asked.

Lao proverb

all things are possible to him that believeth.

Mark 9:23

to **burn always** with a hard, gemlike flame, **that's success** in life.

Robert W. Marks

the main thing
is that you
hear life's
music
everywhere.
most people
hear only its
dissonances.

Theodor Fontane

loyalty to petrified opinion **never** yet broke a chain or **freed** a human **soul.**

Mark Twain

the crucial disadvantage of aggression, competitiveness, and skepticism as characteristics is that these qualities cannot be turned off at five o'clock.

Margaret Halsey

he who laughs – lasts.

Wilfrid Peterson

good **humor is the best** article of dress one can wear in society.

Wm. Makepeace Thackeray

it doesn't hurt to

be optimistic.

you can always cry later.

Lucimar Santos de Lima

you're never fully dressed until you wear a smile.

Charley Willey

the universe is change; our life is what our thoughts make of it.

Marcus Aurelius

the clearest sign of wisdom is continued cheerfulness.

Michel Eyquem de Montaigne

we are all
happy
if we
only knew it.

Dostoevsky

To completely trust in God is to be like a child who knows deeply that even if he does not call for the mother, the mother is totally aware of his condition and is looking after him.

al-Ghazzali

It is the mind that makes one wise or ignorant, bound or emancipated. One is holy because of his mind, one is wicked because of his mind, one is a sinner because of his mind, and it is the mind that makes one virtuous. So he whose mind is always fixed on good requires no other practices, devotion, or spiritual exercises.

Sri Ramakrishna

the greatest
treasure
next to
God is a
good
will
in this world:
even if all
has been lost,
by it
all
can be
regained.

Silesius

before man is
life and death,
good
and evil;
that which
he shall
choose
shall be
given him.

Ecclesiasticus, xv. 18

The magnetic needle always points toward the north, and hence it is that the sailing vessel does not lose her course.

So long as the heart of man is directed towards God, he cannot be lost in the ocean of worldliness.

Sri Ramakrishna

That which is
Bliss is the Self.
Bliss and the Self are
not distinct and
separate but are
one and
identical.

And That
alone is real.

Ramana Maharshi

for all your ills,
I give you
laughter.

Rabelais

laugh.

laughter is
immeasurable.
be joyful though
you have
considered all
the facts.

Wendell Berry

where you
look **is**
where you
go.

**There it is.
I don't believe in
anything, but I'm always glad
to wake up in the morning.
It doesn't depress me.
I'm never depressed.
My basic nervous system is
filled with this optimism.
It's mad, I know, because it's
optimism about nothing.
I think of life as meaningless
and yet it excites me.
I always think something
marvelous is about to happen.**

Francis Bacon

the last of the human freedoms is to choose one's attitude in any given set of circumstances; to choose one's own way.

Viktor Frankl

the sun
is always
shining
someplace.

Muhammad Ali

it takes a
joyful
sound
to make de
world go
round.

Bob Marley

accentuate the
positive,
that's what I say.
it's a trick, but it
works.

Jack Nicholson

your grief lasted
so long. **look!**
healing
is here.

your door was
locked. **look!**
here is
the key.

Rumi

Chapter Two

Tend your own garden.

Here is an extremely abbreviated list of the things in life that you cannot control: Your kids. Your parents. Your friends. Your boyfriend, girlfriend, date, lover or spouse. The cloud over the hammock. Weather in general. Terrorism, brush fires, blowing trash. What your dad thinks of you. Who your next door neighbor votes for. What time in the morning your neighbor empties a box full of empty bottles into the metal trash can twenty-two feet from your bedroom window. What people say about you. What people think about you. What people think and say in general. The stock market. The fate of the Boston Red Sox. The percentage of your daughter's skin that's showing after she gets to school and stuffs whatever you made her put on this morning into the bottom of her locker. Politics, politicians, and hanging chads. Flu, food poisoning, sprained ankles, heart attacks, cancer, brain tumors, the length of the line at the DMV, your ex, your boss, middle management, what they decide back in Chicago, the guy in the car behind you, nitwits, sex, death, taxes, the remote, and God. And that's the *short* list.

**Here is the complete
list of the things
in life that you
can control:
You.**

You can go on with this chapter from here if you want, but there isn't a great deal more that needs to be said. If you get what I'm saying, please feel free to skip ahead and get on with your life. If you'd prefer to stay and quibble about it, okay: you can control dinnertime (sort of), whether or not your clothes are pressed (usually), and the temperature of a room — as long as it's in *your* house, you're in charge, the gas or electricity is functioning, and you have a locked thermostat whose key is hidden in an undisclosed secure location. Otherwise, this is all you got, darling: you and *your* attitude, thoughts, and actions.

To hold any other view is pure folly. I'll say it in the most direct terms: If you want to try to micro-manage the world, you're on the wrong track, you're going to fail, and you're going to be miserable.

Why not let it all go and realize the pure freedom, simplicity, and joy of tending nothing but the garden of your own life, spirit, and soul? I don't mean that you quit your job, abandon your family, and disengage from human affairs. I mean this: accept, *deeply and permanently, that your life is a wave on an immense universal ocean of chaos, change, and unpredictability, and accept that you can't direct either the wave or the ocean*. Your job is to surf. Get up in the morning, stretch, smile, wax your board, paddle, and ride, dude! Live simply, live clean, live kindly, live well.

Don't go anywhere, I beg you!
The sun you are looking for is
inside you.
Rumi

Are you still laboring under the illusion that your happiness is determined by outside factors? Do you believe that who you're married to, the climate you live in, the amount of education or money or stuff you have, your race or gender, or any other circumstance of your life has a lot of bearing on your personal happiness? I am happy to tell you that you are wrong.

This is what psychologists and social scientists who have researched the effect of those things on our happiness will tell you: All those factors *combined* can swing your happiness up or down by no more than about 10%.

If you think I'm lying, read the research. In the course of your reading, you might even stumble across this amazing fact: People who are disabled or seriously ill report themselves as *happier* than the general population. In other words, people from whom virtually everything has been taken except the self, find joy in what is left: the self.

Stop looking outside.

There's probably a dog peeing on your fence, anyway, or the grass on the other side of it is greener than your own. There's *always* a nicer car out there, and psychological research shows that the people who are always looking at it and fretting about it are measurably unhappier than those who accept their lot. Similarly, there's *always* someone in your life who you're deeply convinced would benefit from having you manage their world. *Fuhgeddaboutit.*

Tending your own garden is also what you're going to *have* to do if you're going to be successful at the master principle and be positive, because the world is a big place, full of all kinds of influences and weather, and so is your soul. Once you determine to become a positively valent person, you may find that you have your hands full for a while. Someone steps on your toe, or dents your fender, and you may have work to do to maintain your positive valence. Your boss barks at you, and your attention to yourself will likely be required if you're going to remain calm and positive. Some sinister synapse of self-sabotage fires in your brain, and you're going to need to stop and listen to it, argue with it, and find a less destructive way to be inside your own mind.

All that work aside, there is also tremendous pleasure in tending your own garden. Just as the soul is a big place, it is an exotically beautiful place. There are lovelinesses tucked away in the quiet corners of your self that are sweeter than anything that a new Lexus or lover can bring. Listen to the wise ones:

The point in life is to know what's enough — why envy those otherworld mortals?

With the happiness held in one inch-square heart you can fill the whole space between heaven and earth.

Gensei

Correcting oneself is correcting the whole world. The sun is simply bright. It doesn't correct anyone. Because it shines, the whole world is full of light. Transforming yourself is a means of giving light to the whole world.

Ramana Maharshi

the **real** voyage of
discovery
lies not in seeking
new landscapes, but
in having new eyes.

Marcel Proust

We must become alone, so utterly alone, that we withdraw into our innermost self. It is a way of bitter suffering. But then our solitude is overcome and we are no longer alone, for we find that our innermost self is the spirit, that it is God, the indivisible. And suddenly we find ourselves in the midst of the world, yet undisturbed by its multiplicity, for in our innermost soul we know ourselves to be one with all being.

Hermann Hesse

a person has
two legs and
one sense
of humor.
if you're faced
with the
choice,
it's better to
lose a leg.

Charles Lindner

live
as you will
wish to
have lived
when you are
dying.

Christian Gellert

a good conscience is a continual feast.

Robert Burton

don't compromise yourself.

you're all you've got.

Janis Joplin

think for yourself and let others enjoy the right to do the same.

Voltaire

don't mourn, organize.

Joe Hill

Luck affects everything;
let your hook
always be cast.

In the stream where you
least expect it,
there will be fish.

Ovid

always do right.

this will gratify some people, and astonish the rest.

Mark Twain

**When the mind
is at peace,
the world too is at peace.**

**Nothing real,
nothing absent.
Not holding on to reality,
not getting stuck
in the void,**

**You are neither holy nor
wise, just an ordinary
fellow who has
completed his work.**

Layman P'ang

I have lived on
the lip of insanity,
wanting to know
reasons, knocking on
a door. It opens.

I've been knocking
from the inside!

Rumi

Chapter Three

Exercise your will.

The wise don't expect to find life worth living. they make it that way.

Each and every one of us has a will, as surely as we have legs to walk on or arms to hug with. It may not be as apparent to the eye, but it's there. And it has to be exercised, just like the rest of you does, if you are to be a happy person.

The notion of will has gone somewhat out of fashion, to be sure. In the culture of negativity that surrounds us, people lay the blame for their troubles everywhere but at their own feet. I certainly did: "My mommy let me get run over by a car and that's why I hurt all the time! My Hollywood agent didn't get my films made because he sucked! I'm boozing it up because my ex-wife is such a demon!" — and blabbity blah blah blah, on and on it went. What it kept me from was this: acknowledging that I had a will and could use it to make my life good and positive and happy.

By the will art thou lost,
by the will art thou found,
By the will art thou free,
captive and bound.
Angelus Silesius

The vigorous exercise of your will is essential in the pursuit of happiness. Creating and maintaining a positive valence? Purely a matter of will. First you must exercise your will to honestly look at and evaluate your present valence. If it's negative, you must exercise your will to change it; if it's partially positive, you have to exercise your will to perfect it. When the challenges to your positivity come — and come they will — you have to exercise your will to stay positive. Most importantly, when your own busy little mind tries to attack your state of positive well-being — and if you're human, it will do this — that is the time when exercising your will is most crucial.

Most folks are about as happy
as they make up their minds to be.
Abraham Lincoln

For me, and I think for most people, riding herd on my own darkest tendencies is the toughest part of all. Somehow when self-pity or self-hatred or sadness assert themselves, I seem to want to forget that I even *have* a will — and when I've forgotten that, I don't have one anymore. It's like the tail you used to possess: merely, barely a memory.

Tending your own garden also demands the exercise of your will. Our eyes, and our minds, are prone to wandering, and somehow it's easier to look at one's kid or father or lover and see the source of a problem than it is to see it in yourself. It is the exercise of will that brings our attention back home, where it belongs, and it is the exercise of will that enables us to do the pruning and tilling and planting we need to do in our own soul gardens to make them healthy and beautiful and happy.

Further, most of what is worthwhile in life comes to us through the exercise of our wills. Sunrise, sunset, fresh peaches — these are gifts from the gods. But wisdom? Attained through the exercise of will. Love? Beyond infatuation, also an exercise of will. Justice? Will. Temperance? Will! Kindness and decency, true friendship, accomplishment — all will.

Making a happy life for yourself is a matter of making one good and willful choice after another. In the beginning, there must be the will toward happiness itself. As Seneca said,

**To wish to progress is the
largest part of progress.**

Many people are so unfamiliar with their wills that they hardly ever exercise them, and hardly notice when they do, thus depriving themselves of the pleasure of ownership and use. It is a great achievement and a profound empowerment to *consciously* exercise your will – to say, "I am going to make a good and positive life for myself" and to act to make it happen. Practiced consciously, the exercise of will soon becomes reflexive and automatic – just as the instinct to blame and complain may once have been in, er, idiots like myself. The most powerful tool you own for building a happy life is your will. Exercise it.

life
shrinks or
expands
in proportion
to one's
courage.

Anais Nin

Our deepest fear is not that we are inadequate.
Our deepest fear is that
we are powerful beyond measure.
It is our light, not our darkness,
that most frightens us.
We ask ourselved, who am I to be brilliant,
gorgeous, talented, fabulous?
Actually, who are you not to be?
You are a child of God.
Your playing small does not serve the world.
There is nothing enlightening about shrinking
so that other people won't feel
unsure around you.
We were born to make manifest
the glory of God that is within us.
It is not just in some of us; it is in everyone.
As we let our light shine,
we unconsciously give other people
permission to do the same.
As we are liberated from our own fear,
our presence automatically liberates others.

Nelson Mandela

even the highest towers
begin from the ground.

Chinese Saying

a **diamond**
is a chunk of **coal**
that made **good**
under **pressure.**

Anon.

it's not the size of the dog in the fight, it's the size of the fight in the dog.

Southern Saying

I never had a policy. I just tried to
do my best
every day.

Abraham Lincoln

I'm not happy,
I'm cheerful.
There's a difference.
A happy woman has
no cares
at all.
A cheerful woman has
cares but has learned
how to deal
with them.

Beverly Sills

courage
is resistance to fear,
mastery
of fear, not absence
of fear.

Mark Twain

facing it –
always facing it! –
that's the way to
get through.
face it!

Joseph Conrad

One is always seeking the touchstone that will dissolve one's deficiencies as a person and as a craftsman.

And one is always bumping up against the fact that there is none except hard work, concentration, and continued application.

Paul William Gallico

some pursue
happiness.
others
create it.

Anon.

sentiment without action is the ruin of the soul.

Edward Abbey

it is not because things are difficult that we do not dare; it is because we do not dare that they are difficult.

Lucius Annaeus Seneca

When any disturbing news is brought you, bear this in mind, that news cannot affect anything within the region of the will.

Epictetus

His mother had often said, "When you choose an action, you choose the consequences of that action.

She had emphasized the corollary of this axiom even more vehemently: when you desired a consequence, you had damned well better take the action that would create it.

Lois McMaster Bujold

don't let what you cannot do interfere with what you can do.

John Wooden

fall seven times. stand up eight.

Japanese proverb

see the lantern, trim its wick, fill it with oil!

don't say you'll act tomorrow,

tomorrow — tomorrow is already gone.

Rumi

the more you
strive to
reach
the place of splendor,
the more the
invisible
angels
reach to
help you.

Rumi

The human body, at peace with itself, is more precious than the rarest gem. Cherish your body, it is yours this one time only. The human form is won with difficulty, and is easy to lose. All worldly things are brief, like lightning in the sky. This life you must know as the tiny splash of a raindrop, a thing of beauty which disappears even as it comes into being. Therefore, set your goal. Make use of every day and night to achieve it.

Tsong Khapa

you must
concentrate upon and
consecrate
yourself
wholly to
each day,
as though a fire
were raging in
your hair.

Deshimaru

Chapter Four

Be grateful.

**Most people think that
if they become happy,
they'll become grateful.
But it works the
other way around.
William Baker**

I had the privilege for some years of participating in ceremonies of worship with Native American people. My friend William Baker, a Dakota Sioux from the Ft. Peck Reservation in northeastern Montana, graciously invited me to join in numerous peyote and sweat lodge ceremonies with him and people from tribes all over the United States.

If you have ever visited a reservation like Ft. Peck, you know that I am telling the truth when I say that no one in our country has less, or lives in more miserable conditions, than Indian people. And if you have ever heard the prayers offered in their ceremonial tepees and sweat lodges, you know that there are no more grateful people anywhere. Gratitude is as fundamental to their way of living as breathing is to ours.

Every spiritual tradition of significance in the history of the world has recognized gratitude as not only a core value but a principal practice of good living. Religious people are consistently shown in psychological research data to be happier, healthier, and more satisfied with their lives than others. (You don't have to believe in any particular version of a god to benefit, either; any version of hope and faith has the effect.)

Gratitude is not only
the greatest of virtues,
but the parent
of all others.
Cicero

If you have ever known a deeply grateful human being, this is immediately understandable to you. A person who is filled with gratitude is also inevitably filled with wisdom, goodness, forgiveness, and — lo and behold! — happiness. And the social sciences are catching up with what religion and common sense tell us. Numerous studies done in recent years have shown the effects of grateful living, and they are not small: people who are habitually grateful are happier, healthier, and more successful than others — and it appears from the research that the gratitude causes the happiness, health, and success, rather than the reverse.

In this vein, Dr. Martin Seligman reports that his associates Robert Emmon and Mike McCullough directed three groups of people to keep a daily dairy. One g[illegible] assigned to record the things that they were gratefu[illegible] second to note the things that annoyed them, and a thir[illegible] set down whatever they wished. The people who kept a grat-itude journal showed dramatic increases in self-reported joy, happiness, and satisfaction with life.

Fall into His arms with thanks
and you'll weep like the sky;
refuse Him your thanks
and you'll freeze like the snow.
Rumi

If you don't see that you have anything to be grateful for, your focus is misplaced. Begin to consciously practice grati-tude: make a list every morning and every night of the things you're grateful for now. The simple act of committing your gratitude to paper is tremendously powerful. Positivity, grat-itude, and happiness – is there any difference between them?

o imagines that bliss is
fe is going to waste a lot
ning around shouting
he's been robbed.
that most putts don't
st beef is tough, most
children grow up to be just
people, most successful marriages
require a high degree of mutual
toleration, and most jobs are more
often dull than otherwise.

Life is like an old-time rail journey — delays, sidetracks, smoke, dust, cinders, and jolts, interspersed only occasionally with beautiful vistas and thrilling bursts of speed. The trick is to thank God for letting you have the ride.

Jenkin Lloyd Jones

be
glad
of life because
it gives you the
the chance to
love
and to
work
and to
play and to
look up at
the stars.

Henry van Dyke

gratitude is never lost. if not reciprocated, it will flow back and **soften** and purify the **heart.**

Washington Irving

gratitude
for the abundance
you have received is
the best insurance
that the
abundance
will continue.

Vernon

find expression
for a sorrow,
and it will
become dear to you.
find
expression
for a joy,
and you will
intensify its ecstasy.

Oscar Wilde

three things in life are important. the first is to be grateful. the second is to be grateful. the third is to be grateful.

Henry James

you **pray** in your distress and in your need; would that you might **pray** also in the fullness of your **joy** and in your **abundance.**

Kahlil Gibran

There is a
polish for everything
that takes away rust; and
the polish of the heart is
gratitude to God.

Muhammad

Patience has three stages. First, the servant ceases to complain; this is the stage of repentance. Second, the Sufi becomes satisfied with what is decreed; this is the rank of the ascetic. Third, the servant comes to love whatever the Lord does with him; this is the stage of the true friends of God.

Abu Talib al-Maaki

Open your eyes and you will see at last – He is walking in your garden like the breeze at dawn.

Rumi

What a
wonderful
life
I've had!

I only wish
I'd realized it
sooner.

Colette

**If you walk toward Him,
He comes to you running.**

Muhammad

He's here, invisible but
absolute.
He makes the world grow
fragrant.

Rumi

Give thanks in all circumstances, for this is God's will.

1 Thessalonians 5:18

give thanks and praises!

Bob Marley

Chapter Five

Practice forgiveness.

Forgiveness benefits both the giver and the receiver.
John Marks Templeton

I'm going to start with the science here, and I'm going to make it short and sweet: Every study that has ever been done — and there have been scads of them — shows that the practice of forgiveness directly results in better health; less anger, stress, and their related physical and mental illnesses; higher levels of success; a stronger immune system and resistance to illness and disease; lower chances of divorce; and greater overall well-being — *for the forgiver.*

There. That's the end of the chapter. Or it ought to be. And if what I just told you isn't worth a thousand times what you paid for this book in decreased health care bills and increased moments of happiness, I'll eat my shorts.

If you wish to read a great deal more about these studies and their conclusions — and I strongly recommend that you do because *it will cement your understanding of how crucial to your own well-being it is that you practice forgiveness* — then go to www.forgiving.org. That's the website of the Campaign for Forgiveness Research, which was started by Dr. Everett Worthington, and you can find links there to all sorts of articles about the benefits of forgiveness. Dr. Worthington is the chair of the department of psychology at the University of Virginia and the leading researcher and author on the topic of forgiveness in the world. In his book, *Five Steps to Forgiveness*, he teaches a five-step process of forgiveness which I recommend you learn today, never forget, and practice now and forever. He calls it **REACH**:

Recall the hurt
Empathize with the person who hurt you
Altruistically decide to forgive
Commit publicly to forgiving
Hold on to forgiveness

Interestingly, research shows that older people are more likely to forgive. They're also the group that reports the highest overall well-being and happiness. That's not a coincidence.

Research also shows that victims of incest, violence, and other forms of trauma who go through forgiveness therapy experience significantly better mental health later on than those who do not. That's not a coincidence.

And my grandmother Cincie was not a coincidence. Cynthia Pace Radcliffe was born poor in Virginia in 1898, married young and poor to a husband who died early, worked her skinny butt off raising five children alone in poverty, and died poor in 1980, just after I graduated from college. And I'll tell you something else about her: in her old age, Cincie was as close to enlightened as anyone I've ever known. I went to college in the town where she lived, and she was so cool that my college buddies — well-to-do, beer-guzzling, knuckleheaded jocks one and all — used to beg me to take them with me when I went to hang out with her on the front porch of her tiny little duplex at 816 East Amelia Street.

When I say that Cincie was enlightened, I'm not talking about some Californiacated sitting-in-the-lotus-posture Buddhist version. I'm talking about what I call "rocking chair enlightenment": she was just a person you could spend hours with, sitting on that porch talking, perhaps playing a few hands of cards, and it would be the best time you had all week. She'd say a few dozen awfully wise things, in the simplest fashion, without ever looking like she was trying. She'd make you laugh every thirty seconds at something about life or people, and she herself always laughed the loudest and longest. The minute you left, you already wished you were back on that porch.

She wasn't always like that. Most of her life she was fierce — *mean*, even. She had a razor sharp tongue, an iron will, a leather belt, and a willingness to use all three on anyone who got in her way. She was as different from this in her late life as the current George Foreman is from the young George Foreman. When my mom asked her how she accomplished this transformation, she said, "I sat right out there on that porch for two years and consciously forgave every single person I ever thought had done anything to me."

This is my beloved grandmother, Cincie. You can't tell me, and you couldn't tell her, that forgiveness doesn't lead to happiness.

The old law about 'an eye for an eye' leaves everybody blind.

Martin Luther King, Jr.

you can't hold
a man down
without staying
down with him.

Booker T. Washington

treat **people** as if they were what they should be, and you help them **become** what they are **capable** of becoming.

Goethe

No one can make you feel inferior without your consent.

Eleanor Roosevelt

what is noble can be said in any language, and what is mean should be said in none.

Maimonides

that which you meditate upon is that which you become.

Sri Sri Sri

Ras Ravi Bidublyew

forgiveness is the finding again of a lost possession — hatred an extended suicide.

Friedrich Schiller

It is happier to be sometimes cheated than not to trust.

Samuel Johnson

the art of being wise is the art of knowing what to overlook.

William James

I would rather
be the man
who bought the
Brooklyn Bridge
than the one
who sold it.

Will Rogers

The test of a man's or woman's breeding is how they behave in a quarrel.

George Bernard Shaw

You can no more win a war than you can win an earthquake.

Jeannette Rankin

no man should
judge unless he
asks himself in
absolute
honesty
whether in a similar
situation he might not
have done the same.

Viktor Frankl

it is easy enough to
be friendly
to one's friends. but to
befriend
the one who regards
himself as your
enemy is the
quintessence
of true religion.
the other is mere
business.

Mahatma Gandhi

nonviolence is a weapon of the strong.

Mahatma Ghandi

do you think the universe is agitated?

go into the desert at night

and look out at the stars. this practice should answer the question.

Lao Tzu, *Hua hu Ching*

**people who fight
fire with fire
usually end
up with
ashes.**

Abigail van Buren

Out beyond ideas of wrongdoing and right-doing, there is a field. I'll meet you there. When the soul lies down in that grass, the world is too full to talk about. Ideas, language, even the phrase *each other* doesn't make any sense.

Rumi

Chapter Six

Have a calling.

Work is much more fun than fun.
Noel Coward

Think you'd be happier if you won the lottery and never had to work again? You wouldn't. Careful studies have shown that lottery winners experience a spike of giddiness and then return to whatever their regular level of happiness was before they won a fortune. Money is like drugs, masturbation, and candy — a temporary pleasure at best, and a direct route to unhappiness (or blisters) if pursued obsessively.

Think you'd be happier in the long run if you got a new job, fatter check, more recognition for what you do? You wouldn't. We humans live on something that psychologists call the "hedonic treadmill", which means that in terms of happiness we quickly adjust to the good things that happen to us. A new title, more money, bigger house, plusher car, corner office, a few more wives for Osama — they're all a delight for only a little while. Then we're back where we started, happiness-wise, and we begin looking around for the next hit. The hedonic treadmill is why Donald Trump is still greedy for fur sinks and fame after all these years.

What *would* make you happier is having a calling.

A calling is a focus for your life, probably but not necessarily work-related, which (a) allows you to exercise your strength and skills, and (b) has deep meaning for you beyond money or status.

A calling is the kind of work in which you are challenged, in which you use aptitudes and proficiencies unique to you, in which you lose yourself, and in which time and money fall away and you are doing the thing for the love of doing it. You enter into that state about which the psychologist Mihaly Csikszentmihalyi wrote an entire book, *Flow* — a state that is simultaneously demanding and rewarding, productive and pleasurable.

Flow is immediately apparent in artists — a singer in the throes of song, a painter lost in her picure, a dancer who, as Jim Harrison puts it in his gorgeous poem "Homily", "whirls so hard everything he *is* flies off." But it's also enjoyed by the person feeding the homeless, building a house or website or bicycle, sweeping the halls of the elementary school, sewing, cooking, flying, floating a river, washing cars, *whatever.* Give your strengths and skills a place to express themselves, and you have flow. Add meaning to the equation — some way in which what you do benefits others, be they your family, your community, the world at large — and you have a calling.

How do *you* find *yours*? I suggest you look at two things: what your strengths and skills are, and what you care about. Then find a way to marry them in some kind of pursuit or practice. Because I'm a good writer and I love provoking myself and others into leading richer, fuller lives, my calling is making books like this one. My friend Brian Doubleday loves film and loves ideas, and his calling is to find a way to marry them. Sometimes he makes a series for public television, other times he produces a big feature film like "Instinct" with Anthony Hopkins and Cuba Gooding, Jr. My friend Scot MacInnis has huge, strong, soft hands and a huge, strong, soft heart, so his calling is to be the best massage therapist in Boulder, Colorado.

My dad, Bud Walker, fell in love with aviation at the age of 12 in 1937, spent his life teaching people to fly every imaginable kind of airplane, seaplane, and helicopter, and at age 78 is still practicing his calling by taking young people up to fly and performing an advanced aerobatic routine in airshows. My big sister Laurie was getting a Ph.D. in botanical genetics until she discovered that what she was really good at and loved was not monitoring electron microscopes and computers in a sterile laboratory, but rather people and messing about with plants and dirt. Now her calling is directing the Botanical Gardens at the University of South Florida and creating all sorts of outreach programs to give the folks in her community a lively relationship with the living things in their yards, gardens, and general environment.

You don't necessarily have to get paid for your calling. My mom's calling is, in a word, kindness. She has practiced it by caring well for her family and showering love, attention, and assistance on orphans, Vietnamese refugees, and people learning to read. Whenever she encounters a person in need, she steps up to the plate. It's a beautiful calling and of enormous value to the world even though it doesn't bring her a cent.

If you really need some help in figuring out what yours might be, take a look at the "Resources" section of my website, www.behappybooks.com. Probably you already have a pretty good seat-of-the-pants idea what might constitute a calling for you. Either way, go to it. There's happiness there.

If men believe,
as I do, that
this present
earth is the
only heaven,
they will strive all
the more to make
heaven of it.

Sir Arthur Keith

be ashamed to die until you have won one victory for humanity.

Horace Mann

...to **labor**
eighty years in a notch
of eternity is nothing
too tiresome, enormous
repose after,
enormous
repose before,
the flash of activity.

Robinson Jeffers

we think
work with
the brain is
more worthy than
work with
the hands.
nobody who works
with his hands
could ever fall
for this.

E.F. Schumacher

the labor of a human being is not a commodity or an article of commerce. you can't weigh the soul of a man with a bar of pig iron.

Samuel Gompers

the important thing in **life** is not the **triumph** but the **struggle.**

Pierre de Coubertin

If all the rich men in the world divided up their money amongst themselves, there wouldn't be enough to go round.

Christina Stead

Making
money ain't nothing
exciting to me.
You might be able to buy a little better booze than the wino on the corner, but you get sick just like the next cat, and
when you die
you're just as graveyard dead.

Louis Armstrong

Reconsider your definitions.

We are prone to judge success by the index of our salaries or the size of our automobiles rather than by the quality of our service and relationship to mankind.

Martin Luther King, Jr.

many persons have
a wrong idea
of what
constitutes true
happiness.
it is not
attained through
self-gratification but
through fidelity to
**a worthy
purpose.**

Helen Keller

Nothing will ever be attempted if all possible objections must be first overcome.

Samuel Johnson

the Wright brothers
flew right through
the smoke screen of
impossibility.

Charles Franklin Kettering

life consists not in holding good cards, but in playing well those you do hold.

Josh Billings

My daily affairs are quite ordinary; but I'm in total harmony with them. I don't hold on to anything, don't reject anything; nowhere an obstacle or conflict. Who cares about wealth and honor? Even the poorest thing shines. My miraculous power and spiritual activity: drawing water and carrying wood.

Layman P'ang

Chapter Seven

Love.

Your mother and father were playing at love.
They came together and you showed up!
Don't question what love can do:
See the colors of the world.
Rumi

I worked very hard when preparing this book to reduce the number of principles I would share to the absolute minimum. I didn't want to leave anything out that could help you in creating a happy life, but I wanted there to be just a handful of principles so that you could remember them, recite them to yourself every morning and evening, and use them - *really* use them — forever. I was pretty satisfied with seven.

And if you noticed, I expressed the first six as simply as possible: "Be positive", "Tend your own garden", "Exercise your will", "Give thanks", "Practice forgiveness", "Have a calling". I thought I'd done a pretty good job, but what I discover this morning as I turn to the seventh principle is that pretty much everything that came before is comfortably contained within its four letters: L-O-V-E.

You see what I mean, of course. Cultivating a positive valence, tending your own garden, and exercising your will are ways of loving yourself (and others)! Being grateful, practicing forgiveness, and having a calling are simply ways of loving others (and yourself)! Ah, well — I still think the first six principles are worth specifically remembering and practicing every day.

And the seventh? This one is worth remembering and practicing every minute for the rest of your life, if you live that long. Always remember that an essential component of genuine love is *letting go* — letting go of what happened in the past, letting go of what you hope happens in the future, letting go of all agendas, ideas, and concerns, and simply loving. I find it helpful to remind myself to let go in the same moment I remind myself to love. I hope you will, too. Now go to work.

Love
your own sacred body, soul, and self

Love
someone else

Love
God or a reasonable facsimile

Love
your friends and family

Love
your home

Love
music

Love
sunshine

Love
rain

Love
pain

Love
sadness

Love
beauty

Love
the light inside the darkness

Love
everything that has been

Love
everything that is

Love
everything that will be

Love
love

because if you love love love, loves you, too.

Bruce Cockburn

what goes around, comes around.

Richard Pryor

there is no religion without love,

and people may talk as much as they like about their religion, but if it does not teach them to be good and kind to man and beast, it is all a sham.

Anna Sewell

Let us endeavor so to live that when we come to die even the undertaker will be sorry.

Mark Twain

We often hear of the beauties of old age, but the only old age that is beautiful is the one the man has been long preparing for by living a beautiful life. Every one of us is right now preparing for old age... There may be a substitute somewhere in the world for Good Nature, but I do not know where it can be found. The secret of salvation is this: keep sweet, be useful, and keep busy.

Elbert Hubbard

we are
here to
awaken from
the illusion
of our
separateness.

Thich Nhat Hanh

the
most exquisite
pleasure
is giving
pleasure to others.

Jean de la Bruyere

There is no exercise better for the heart than reaching down and lifting people up.

John Andrew Holmer

if you want others to be happy, practice compassion. if you want to be happy, practice compassion.

The Dalai Lama

where **love** is concerned, even too much is not enough.

Pierre-Augustin Caron de Beaumarchais

a lot of people
are waiting for
Martin Luther King, Jr.
or Mahatma Gandhi
to come back,
but they are gone.
it's up to us.

Marian Wright Edelman

the only remedy for love is to love more.

Henry David Thoreau

How else but through a broken heart may Christ enter in?

Oscar Wilde

you're never too old to become younger.

Mae West

what is **love?** it's like electricity — we don't really know what it is, but it's a **force** that can **light** a room.

Ray Charles

choose in
marriage
only a woman you
would choose in
friendship
were she a man.

Joseph Joubert

we tend to
think of the
erotic
as an easy,
tantalizing
sexual arousal.
I speak of the erotic
as the
deepest life
force, a force
which moves us
toward living in a
fundamental way.

Audre Lorde

sexual intercourse is

kicking death in the ass

while singing.

Charles Bukowski

You discover real true love at the moment when you are making love with your partner and realize that all your life together is a single continuous and ongoing act of lovemaking, in the course of which you happen to occasionally disengage bodies altogether for hours at a time. It is not something to which you return — it is something you suddenly find that you have never really left.

Spider and Jeanne Robinson

politics is how you live your life, not whom you vote for.

Jerry Rubin

love is the only law to obey.

Ziggy Marley

**love has come
to transform
and to rule —
stay awake,
heart,
stay awake.**

Rumi

Love is the key that unlocks the door to the ultimate reality.

Dr. Martin Luther King, Jr.

what do we live for if not to make life less difficult for each other?

George Eliot

the best thing against worry is to take care of others right away.

Carl Hilty

One can live at a low flame. Most people do. For some, life is an exercise in moderation (best china saved for special occasions), but given something like death, what does it matter if one looks foolish now and then, or tries too hard, or cares too deeply?

Diane Ackerman

Fasting is a way to save on food. Vigil and prayer is a labor for old folks. Pilgrimage is an occasion for tourism. To distribute bread in alms is something for philanthropists.

Fall in love:

That is doing something!

Ansari

sexual love is the most stupendous fact of the universe, and the most magical mystery our poor blind senses know.

Amy Lowell

Blessed are the man and the woman who have grown beyond their greed and have put an end to their hatred and no longer nourish illusions. But they delight in the way things are and keep their hearts open, day and night. They are like trees planted near flowing rivers, and which bear fruit when they are ready. Their leaves will not fall or wither. Everything they do will succeed.

Psalm I

In all ten directions of the universe, there is just one truth. When we see clearly, all great teachings are the same. What can ever be lost? What can be gained? If we gain something, it was there from the beginning of time. If we lose something, it is hiding somewhere near us. Look: this ball in my pocket: Can you see how priceless it is?

Ryokan

The end of the book...

...is just the beginning of the happy life. I promise you that if you go forth and practice the seven principles I've set down here, you will find yourself happier than you've ever been before, and happy forever. Memorize them, remind yourself of them every morning as soon as you wake up and just before you sleep, work at each one every day. If you like, devote one day a week to really concentrating on one at a time.

Choose whatever method you like, but exercise your will and choose one. Make these principles the foundation of your being and they will reward you in spades. If you try it for a solid year and it doesn't work, write me a letter about what you tried and how it failed, and I'll give you your money back just like I promised up front.

I don't expect I'll ever have to write one of those checks, though. What's in this book works, and works powerfully, if you practice it. It isn't always easy, of course. Life is challenging, and it seems sometimes to rise to the occasion and challenge us more vigorously when we resolve to be positive, to exercise our wills, to forgive. But adult happiness, unlike that of babes, is earned - and all the more deeply felt, once you arrive it, for being so. Jack Kornfield puts it beautifully in *After the Ecstasy, the Laundry*:

> The unfolding of the human heart is artful and mysterious. We might wish the path to enlighten-

ment were orderly and predictable, but the ways of the heart are a landscape discoverable only in the journey. We cannot capture freedom and place it in time. For the mature spirit, freedom is the journey itself. It is like a labyrinth, a circle, a flower's petal-by-petal opening, or a deepening spiral, a dance around the still point, the center of all things. There are always changing cycles: ups and downs, openings and closings, awakenings to love and freedom, often followed by new and subtle entanglements. In the course of this great spiral, we return to where we started again and again, but each time with a fuller, more open heart.

There are turns and turns to the spiral, layers and layers to the onion of your life. Keep turning and peeling. Turn and peel with positivity, will, gratitude, forgiveness, and love. You may never finish. But try to finish today.

So go be happy now. And come and visit me at www.behappybooks.com whenever you like.

Thanks and Praises

One lotus that arises from the muck of living in darkness for a very long time, as I did, is that you come to understand who your true friends are. I wish to make mention here of two of mine, Scot MacInnis and Brian Doubleday, and to thank them from my heart for their steadfastness, their humor, their soul, and their love. I am grateful to you both for so much. You give the word "friend" its deepest meaning, even if you are funny looking.

The blessing of family in my life has been large and has sustained and nourished me when I could not do those things for myself. The loving support of my mother and father, Joan and Bud, and of my sisters Laurie and Julie has been soft, sweet, and unswerving. My grandmother Cynthia Pace Radcliffe left this earth twenty four years ago but has never left my side. Her son Harry Radcliffe, my Uncle Bud, taught me a great deal from a great distance about how to live a positive life, and he did this with almost no words and a large dose of living by gorgeous example. Thank you, Bud.

These two are birds of a feather and belong in the same paragraph: David Lynn Grimes is not only the finest singer and songwriter that I know, but my very own brother. Reta Lawlor, I'd marry you if you would have me.

Closer to my own hearth, I have a teacher and friend whose name is Sasha. She has led two consecutive lives in my presence disguised as a white standard poodle. Her teachings on love, humor, gentleness, fidelity, and positivity lead me to believe that the difference between God and dog is minimal if it exists at all.

Finally, my most heartfelt hug and gratitude are for my beloved daughter Sofia, whose life has expanded my own beyond description, whose sweetness gave mine a reason to return, whose light was a beacon in the dark and is now simply the sun. Teacher, friend, comedienne, snuggling partner, and the boonest of companions — I love you now and forever with my whole heart, Little Rabbit.

Until you become a
rebirth, you won't know
what that is.

It's the same with anything.
You don't understand
until you are
what you're trying
to understand.

Become reason,
and you'll know it perfectly.
Become love
and be a burning wick
at the center of yourself.

I would make this
very plain,
if someone were ready
for what I have to tell.
Figs are cheap around here!
Mystical knowledge
is easy to come by.
All you need is just to arrive,
as a bird who loves figs
lights in a fig tree.

Rumi